SERIES EDITOR	DAVID SALARIYA
BOOK EDITOR	APRIL McCROSKIE
CONSULTANT	DR GERALD LEGG

First American Edition 1997 by
Franklin Watts
A Division of Grolier Publishing
Sherman Turnpike
Danbury, CT 06816

Library of Congress Cataloging-in-Publication Data
Steedman, Scott.
 Our Planet / written by Scott Steedman: illustrated by Carolyn Scrace.
   p. cm. – (Worldwise: 20)
 Includes index.
 Summary: Provides a simple introduction to the origin, composition,
physical features, and inhabitants of planet Earth.
   ISBN 0-531-14439-9 (lib. ed.). – ISBN 0-531-15316-9 (pbk.)
   1. Earth – Juvenile literature. [1. Earth.]   I. Scrace, Carolyn,
ill. II. Title. III. Series.
QB631.4.S72 1997   96-27734
551– dc20   CIP
                                                                    AC

Printed in Belgium

our planet

Written by
SCOTT STEEDMAN
Illustrated by
CAROLYN SCRACE

Series Created & Designed by
DAVID SALARIYA

FRANKLIN WATTS
A Division of Grolier Publishing
New York•London•Hong Kong
Sydney• Danbury, Connecticut

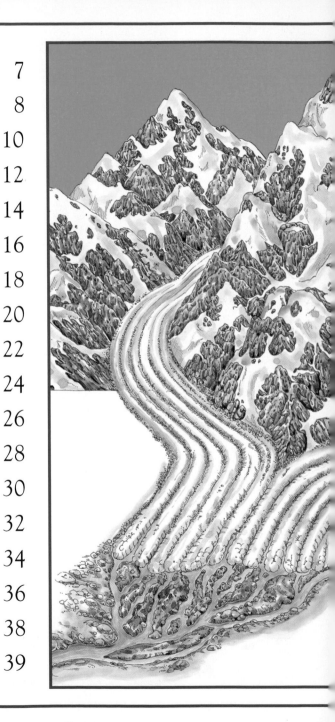

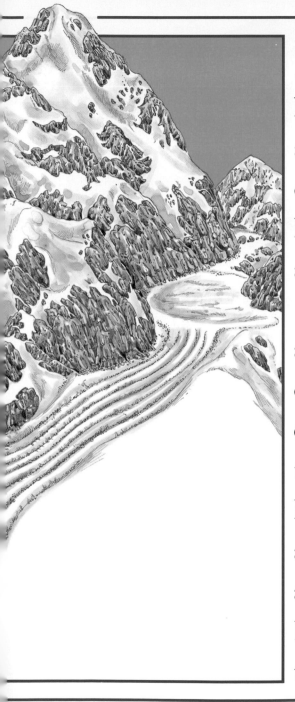

Planet Earth is your home.

You may live in a shack in a forest or a high-rise building in a city. But beneath your feet is planet Earth. Its mountains, rivers, plants and animals, are all around you.

People have always wondered about our planet. Where did it come from? How are seas and deserts formed? What makes the sky blue or the wind blow? How did life begin? Science has answered most of these questions, as you will find out in this book. But there are some questions about the Earth which are still mysteries.

Mercury

Venus

Earth

Mars

Uranus

Jupiter

Saturn

Neptune   Pluto

Milky Way Galaxy

Nicolaus Copernicus of Poland was the first astronomer to guess that the planets spin around the Sun, not the Earth. He published his theory in 1543.

Earth is a round ball spinning in space. It is 7,927 miles (12,757 km) wide and 25,000 miles (40,075 km) around the middle. But this is tiny compared to the Sun. Earth is one of nine planets that spin around this star. Together, they form the solar system. Our galaxy, the Milky Way, contains 100,000 million solar systems. And the universe has millions of other galaxies.

The Earth spins on its axis once every 24 hours. At any moment, about half of the planet faces the Sun, and is in day. The rest is in darkness, or night.

North Pole

Atmosphere

North America

Europe

Africa

South America

Pacific Ocean

Atlantic Ocean

It takes the Earth just over 365 days – one year – to circle the Sun. The angle at which the Earth is tilted causes the seasons. When a part of the Earth is tilted toward the Sun, it enjoys the warmth of summer. But six months later, when it is tilted away from the Sun, it suffers the cold of winter.

Axis

South Pole

The Earth's axis runs through the North Pole and the South Pole.

9

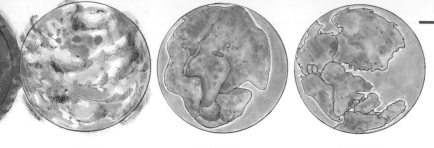

4.5 BYA   1.5 BYA   0.5 BYA   0.2 BYA

4.6 BYA

For almost half of its lifetime, the Earth has been home to different forms of life. Early bacteria formed 3 BYA. Fish go back 410 million years ago (MYA), and dinosaurs lived 240 to 138 MYA.

Scientists believe the universe formed about 15 billion years ago (BYA) in a huge explosion called the Big Bang. About 4.5 BYA, the Earth began to form from a massive cloud of gas and dust. The cloud shrank to form a red-hot ball of rock. The surface cooled and hardened. Volcanoes erupted, letting off gases and steam. The gases became Earth's atmosphere, and this became the air we breathe. The steam became the seas and oceans.

Cooling lava

Large crystals formed by intense heat

1 BYA

Today

About 360 million years ago the land was joined together. It moved slowly and broke apart to form continents.

Cloud of gas and dust

Most of the water on Earth today was released by volcanoes millions of years ago. In the intense heat of eruptions, gases —hydrogen, ammonia, helium, and methane— combined to form steam, which eventually fell to Earth as rain.

Gas from erupting volcanoes also formed the atmosphere, which protects the Earth from the Sun's rays.

Volcanoes covered the Earth for hundreds of millions of years. Clouds blocked out the Sun, and torrential rain fell to Earth.

Newly-formed rocks

Leaf

Shells

Fish

A river carries sediment, like sand and pebbles. When sediment hits the sea, the big particles sink. They form layers and turn to rock as they are buried.

Diamond

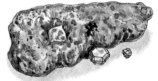

Quartz

Gold

Rocks form

in three ways. Sedimentary rocks are made of particles gathered together by running water, wind and ice. The particles pile up until the pressure turns them into rock. Both igneous and metamorphic rocks are created by heat. The Earth's surface, or crust, is cool and hard. At about 25 miles (40 km) down, the crust meets the mantle. The temperature here is 1,832° F (1000° C). The Earth's core is 6,260° F (4,500° C).

All rocks are mixtures of pure substances called minerals. Many form beautiful crystals. Diamond and gold are rare; quartz is common.

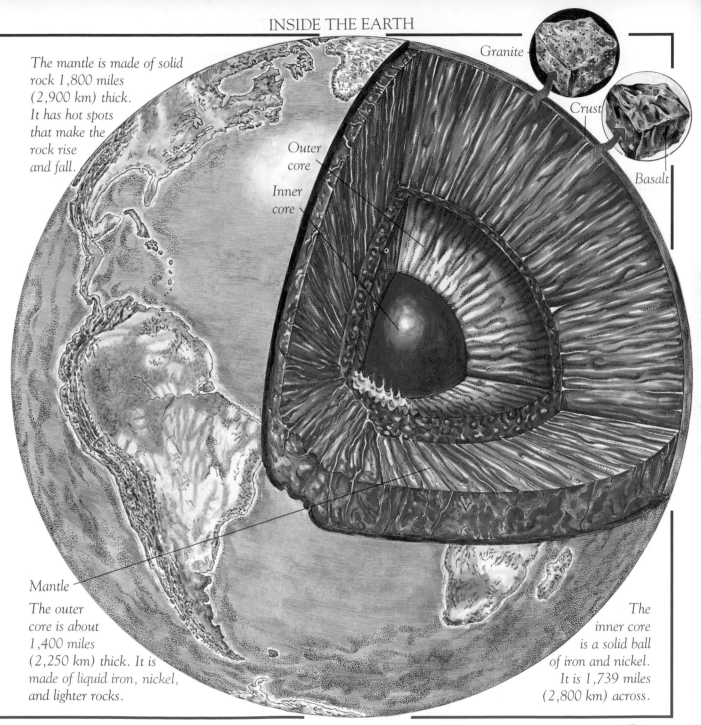

The mantle is made of solid rock 1,800 miles (2,900 km) thick. It has hot spots that make the rock rise and fall.

Granite

Crust

Basalt

Outer core

Inner core

Mantle

The outer core is about 1,400 miles (2,250 km) thick. It is made of liquid iron, nickel, and lighter rocks.

The inner core is a solid ball of iron and nickel. It is 1,739 miles (2,800 km) across.

13

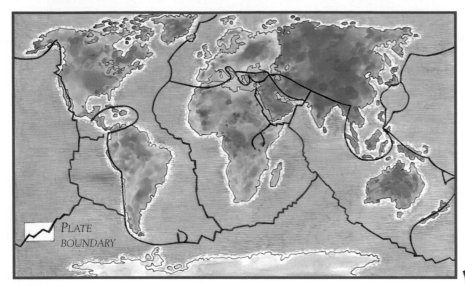

PLATE
BOUNDARY

The main plates float on the liquid rock of the mantle. The currents in the mantle are pushing some plates together, and others apart. This process is called plate tectonics, or continental drift.

Liquid rock causes volcano

The Earth's crust is

divided into moving sections of land and seabed called plates. As two plates move apart, new crust is made. When plates collide, old rocks are forced underground. This creates earthquakes and volcanoes. Earthquakes also occur where plates rub together. These forces move the continents a few inches each year. Over millions of years, they collide and change shape.

At the mid-ocean ridge, hot rock from inside the Earth reaches the surface. It cools and hardens. This pushes the two plates apart.

Mid-ocean ridge

When two plates collide, one is forced down and broken up in the mantle.

Two plates may slide in opposite directions. The pressure creates a fault system. The most famous is the San Andreas Fault in California.

Violent volcano

Fault

Liquid rock rises at ridge

Mountains and volcanoes are created when plates collide.

Plate being pushed down into mantle

Gentle ridge volcano

15

When a volcano erupted on Krakatoa, Indonesia, in 1883, 36,400 people were killed by tidal waves.

An erupting volcano

spouts hot ash and gas into the air. Rivers of lava – red-hot rock – pour down the mountainside. Some volcanoes erupt gently for years. But the most dangerous come to life suddenly. An eruption can blow up a mountain and destroy a town. Dust may be carried around the world.

Crater

A big eruption at sea can form a new island. Whole chains of islands, like the Hawaiian chain, can be created in this way.

Layers of ash and lava from earlier eruptions.

Volcanoes occur because magma – liquid rock inside the Earth – reaches the surface. In gentle eruptions, the magma pours out as lava. In violent eruptions, it is crushed up to form clouds of ash. Millions of tons of new rock may be spilled out in an eruption.

Side 'pipes'

Main 'pipe'

Magma chamber

RICHTER SCALE:

| 0 - 3.0 | 3 - 3.4 | 3.5 - 4.0 | 4.0 - 4.4 | 4.5 - 4.8 | 4.9 - 5.4 |

Feeble:
Earthquakes less than 3.0 can only be felt by a special machine. Above that, leaves tremble on trees.

Slight to moderate:
A few people notice shaking. Door handles jiggle and loose objects rock.

Quite strong to strong:
Most people notice shaking, sleepers are awakened. Trees tremble, tiles and chimneys fall off houses.

An earthquake

can turn a town to rubble. The ground shakes and buildings collapse. Roads are ripped apart, bridges break up and power lines fall down. The shaking may only last for thirty seconds. But fires often start in the rubble, and water pipes may burst. Earthquakes are caused by movements in the Earth's crust. Their size is measured on the Richter scale, from 1 to 12.

Fault lines

Tsunami (tidal wave) caused by earthquake at sea

Volcanoes and earthquakes occur only in areas where plates meet. Some places, like Japan and California, are shaken regularly. Both Tokyo and San Francisco have been hit by big earthquakes this century. The 1923 Tokyo quake killed 100,000 people.

| 5.5 - 6.0 | 6.1 - 6.5 | 6.6 - 7.0 | 7.1 - 7.3 | 7.4 - 8.1 | 8.1+ |

Ruinous to disastrous:
Houses collapse. Roads crack, water
and gas pipes burst. Landslides
occur. Cracks open in the ground.

Very strong to destructive:
Walls of buildings crack under the
strain. Weak buildings collapse.
Stronger structures crumple.

Very disastrous to catastrophic:
Near total destruction.
Few buildings remain standing.
Ground rises and falls in waves.

An earthquake starts underground,
at its epicenter. The shock waves
spread out in all directions.

The waves can be felt by
machines on the other
side of the world.

Focus

Epicentre

The Focus is the
point on the surface
closest to the epicenter.
It is usually the hardest
hit. A deep epicenter means
less damage on the ground.

19

Wind, clouds and rain

are all caused by the Sun heating the Earth.
Hot air rises and cooler air rushes in to
replace it. This moving air is wind.

The Sun's heat also causes water to
evaporate. The water vapor rises into the air,
cooling as it rises. Soon it turns back into
water droplets and a cloud forms.
The cloud darkens – rain is on the way.

*Why is the sky blue?
Because blue light is
scattered by the
atmosphere. Other
colors pass through it,
so it cannot be seen.*

*At sunset or sunrise,
the blue light is
absorbed completely.
Only red is
scattered, so the
sky looks red.*

*Clouds
form where
sea meets land.*

*Water
vapour
rises*

There are many different types of clouds. They are identified by their shape and height, and whether or not they bring rain. The fluffy rain clouds are cumulonimbus. They start to form about 1 mile (1.8 km) above the ground, and reach up to 7 miles (12 km) into the sky.

Cumulonimbus cloud

Mountains force up air, forming clouds and rain.

Rain

Streams

River

Water cycle: Rain flows into rivers, which end in the sea. Water evaporates, forms clouds, and becomes rain again.

Lightning is a giant electric spark. It may leap between clouds, or between a cloud and the ground. Lightning often strikes high points, like tall trees or church steeples. It heats the air suddenly. This makes the air expand, causing a loud crashing sound – thunder.

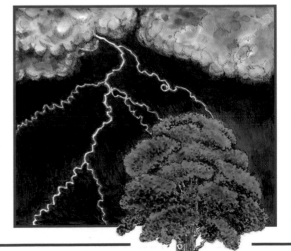

A mountain river, fed by glaciers and melted snow.

High ground

Melting ice

Glacier-fed lake

Waterfall

Gorge

Rapids

Wide, slow river

Mouth of river

Most rivers are formed in the mountains. Here, rain and snow fall to the ground and flow into rushing streams. Glaciers (rivers of ice), lakes and springs also feed mountain streams. Many streams come together to form a big river. Along their paths, streams and rivers wear away the rocks. This creates deep valleys and gorges. In steep spots they become rapids or waterfalls. In the end, all rivers flow into the sea.

A big river is created by many smaller streams and rivers, each one flowing into the next.

A lake is formed when a stream or river is blocked by rock – or a dam (barrier).

Most caves form in limestone, a soft rock. Draining water and rivers dissolve the rock, creating tunnels and chambers. Dripping water, containing dissolved limestone, forms pillars. Stalactites hang from the roof. Stalagmites rise from the floor. Caves are found by the sea, and inside glaciers and volcanoes, too.

Spring

Stalactite

Stalagmite

Waterfall

Lake

Meander

Oxbow lake

Inside a cave

Bay

Sea

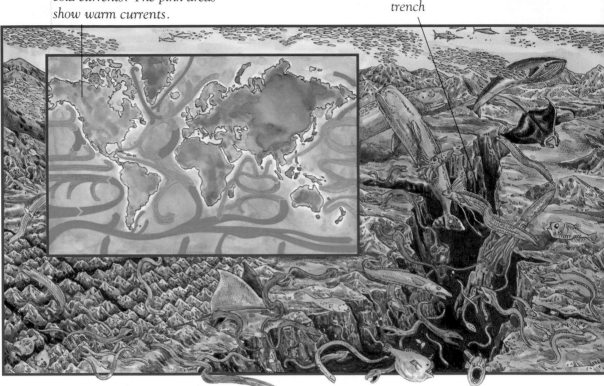

Blue areas on the map show cold currents. The pink areas show warm currents.

Ocean trench

Winds create both waves and currents. Waves travel through the surface of the water until they break onto the beach. Currents may be very deep.

The Blue Planet is the name the first astronauts gave to our planet. This is because seas and oceans cover more than two-thirds of the Earth's surface. From space, it looks blue.

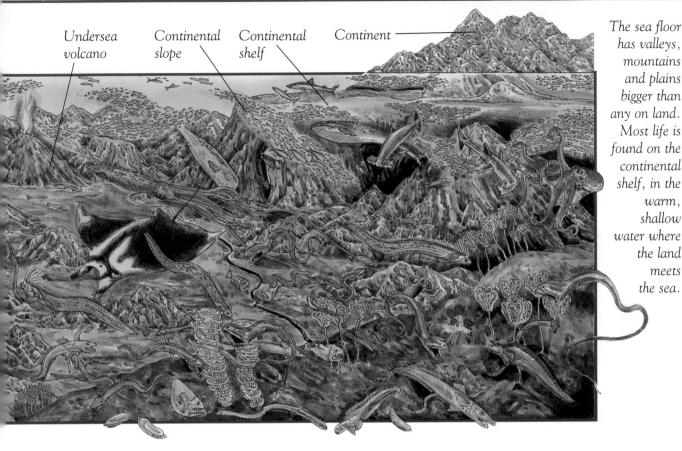

Undersea volcano

Continental slope

Continental shelf

Continent

The sea floor has valleys, mountains and plains bigger than any on land. Most life is found on the continental shelf, in the warm, shallow water where the land meets the sea.

Some experts believe that life began in the seas. A dazzling range of plants and animals still live there. These include the blue whale and the mysterious creatures of the ocean's darkest depths.

Why are seas salty?
Because they are full of dissolved minerals. Some come from the rocks the water washes against. But most come from volcanic eruptions in deep ocean trenches. The Dead Sea in Israel is so salty that people can float on the surface!

Mountains are created by the same forces that move the plates and continents. This takes millions of years. The Earth's highest mountain, Mount Everest in Nepal is 29,028 feet (8,848 m) high. It is still rising.

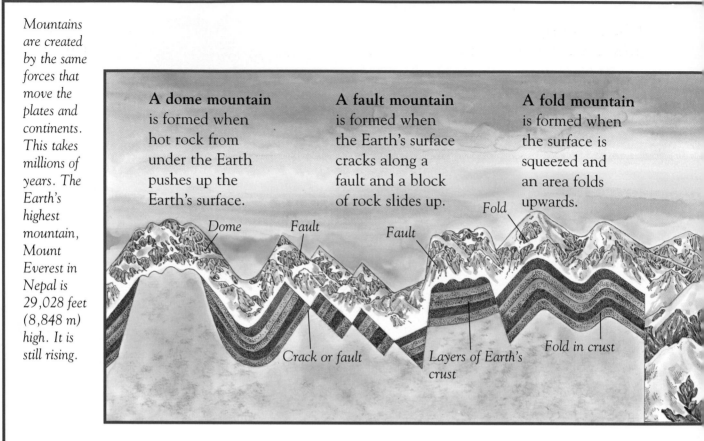

A dome mountain is formed when hot rock from under the Earth pushes up the Earth's surface.

A fault mountain is formed when the Earth's surface cracks along a fault and a block of rock slides up.

A fold mountain is formed when the surface is squeezed and an area folds upwards.

Dome

Fault

Fault

Fold

Crack or fault

Layers of Earth's crust

Fold in crust

Mountains are the highest places on Earth.

Many cold, windy peaks are covered in snow and ice all year round. The snow and ice may form giant rivers of ice, called glaciers, or cause huge snowslides, known as avalanches.

Glacier ice may be 3,280 feet (1,000 m) thick.

Snowy peaks

No trees grow this high up.

When a lot of ice and snow builds up, a glacier is formed. Glaciers move slowly downhill.

Glacier

Crevasses are deep cracks in glaciers.

A moraine is an area where rock has been pushed down a mountain by a glacier.

Two glaciers can meet and join together. Lower down the mountain the air is warmer, so the ice melts. The glacier ends in a stream or a lake of melted water. If the glacier reaches a sea it breaks up to form icebergs.

Avalanche

Streams of melted water

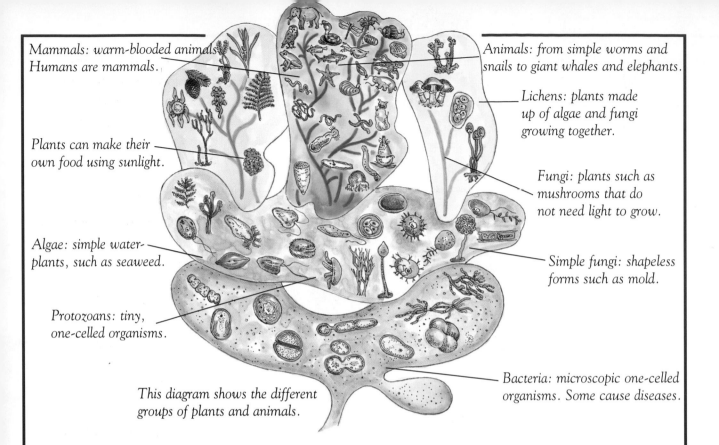

Mammals: warm-blooded animals. Humans are mammals.

Animals: from simple worms and snails to giant whales and elephants.

Plants can make their own food using sunlight.

Lichens: plants made up of algae and fungi growing together.

Fungi: plants such as mushrooms that do not need light to grow.

Algae: simple water-plants, such as seaweed.

Simple fungi: shapeless forms such as mold.

Protozoans: tiny, one-celled organisms.

Bacteria: microscopic one-celled organisms. Some cause diseases.

This diagram shows the different groups of plants and animals.

The first life forms

appeared on Earth 2,000 million years ago. Many new animals have come and gone since. Dinosaurs dominated the land for millions of years. But they died out long ago. Now mammals are the main life forms.

There are millions of different plants and animals on Earth. They can all be put into groups. The biggest animals, including bears, elephants and human beings, are mammals.

Moeritherium Platybelodon Gomphotherium Woolly mammoth Modern elephant

The animals alive today are the ancestors of other kinds that died out long ago. This process of change is called evolution. For example, many types of elephant lived in the past but there are only two kinds on Earth now. The woolly mammoth was much bigger than the modern elephant.

Teeth were 6 inches (15 cm) long

The giant Tyrannosaurus rex dinosaur is the biggest hunter ever found on land. It had tiny hands, and ran standing up.

Pentaceratops, a plant-eater

For 160 million years, dinosaurs ruled the land. The biggest were slow plant-eaters like Brachiosaurus, which weighed around 80 tons. Meat-eaters included Albertosaurus. The smallest dinosaurs, like Compsognathus, were the size of chickens. There were other reptiles, living at the same time, that could fly like birds. Others swam in the seas. Dinosaurs died out about 65 million years ago.

Canopy

Middle layer

The highest trees grow up to 164 feet (50 m).

Forest floor

The biggest jungle is the Amazon of South America. Other jungles are found in Asia, Africa and Australia.

Huge beak for eating fruits and berries

Bright toucan birds are common in South American jungles.

Jungles are thick forests found in the warmest parts of the world. They are home to more kinds of plants and animals than any other habitat.

Jungle trees grow to great heights. Monkeys, snakes and colorful birds live in their highest branches. Leopards and pythons hunt lower down. Antelopes and gorillas feed on the jungle floor.

Parakeet

South American tree boa

Postman butterfly

Three-toed sloth

The jungle is filled with life. As well as big animals, like monkeys and sloths, it is home to frogs, lizards and snakes. Bright birds, such as hummingbirds and parrots, feed on flowers and fruit.

Jungles are crawling with insects. It is almost impossible to count them all. But experts guess that there are more than a million different kinds.

Oasis hummingbird

Coati

Squirrel monkey

Tamandua

Giant armadillo

Bromeliad plant

Red-eyed tree frog

Praying mantis

*The camel is
a desert animal.*

*Desert peoples
travel by camel*

Sand dunes

Deserts are dry places.
They cover one fifth of the
Earth's land surface. It almost
never rains, and the sun shines
all day long. The days are
unbearably hot, but the nights
can be very cold. Many deserts
are covered in sand, which the
wind blows into dunes and
sandstorms. Other deserts are
strewn with barren rock. Water
is scarce, and only the toughest
plants and animals can survive.

DESERTS

Trees may grow in an area, called an oasis, where there is water.

Scorpions look for shade

Living in the desert is a battle for survival. Many animals hide in burrows all day. At night, when the temperature drops, they come out to hunt or search for water.

A gecko is a kind of lizard.

The largest desert is the Sahara. The Gobi Desert, in China, is a cold desert.

The huge ears of the desert fox help it to hear its prey – mice and beetles. They also help it to cool down by giving off heat.

— *Desert fox*

The desert rat is a mouse-like animal, which has big toes to stop it from sinking into the sand.

Long legs for hopping

Desert rat

Earth's desert areas (shown in yellow)

Arctic

Antarctic

TOP; NORTH POLE,
BOTTOM; SOUTH POLE.

The poles are the icy extremes of the Earth. The Arctic is a freezing ocean around the North Pole. The South Pole is in the Antarctic, a vast continent always covered in massive ice sheets. Many animals live in the polar seas.

Young cubs

Paw with long claws

Polar bears are only found in the Arctic. A large bear can weigh 1,763 pounds (800 kg). They are covered in thick white fur, and are excellent swimmers. Their main food is seals. The female gives birth in the middle of winter, in a den in the snow. The cubs stay there, feeding on mother's milk, until spring comes. Then they are ready to learn to hunt.

Weddell seal   Glacier   Adélie penguin

Penguins are only found in the southern hemisphere. They are birds, but none of the 18 different kinds can fly. They are good swimmers, and share the icy seas with seals and whales.

Elephant seal

Tusk

Both poles are covered in sheets of ice all year round. The biggest sheets, in the Antarctic, are more than 1.2 miles (2 km) thick. Around the edges, giant slabs of ice break off and fall into the sea. This is how icebergs are formed.

The walrus is a huge, fat seal. It is only found in the Arctic. Males weigh more than a ton. They use their tusks to clear breathing holes in the ice. Tusks can be 3 feet (1 m) long.

Loggers at work

Mining in a quarry

Logging means cutting down trees. In many countries this causes arguments. Big logging companies turn forests into waste lands to make money. Many local people try to stop the logging.

Save our planet! Earth is the only home that humans have. But we are making a horrible mess of it. Factories and cars pollute (poison) the air we breathe. Dangerous chemicals are dumped in the seas, and tankers spill oil overboard. Forests are cut down to build more houses. All over the world, cities are growing, and nature is losing out.

Many people believe it is time to change our ways. We must stop polluting, and find new ways to live in harmony with the planet, and its plants and animals.

Jet plane

Most planes, buses, trains and cars run on gasoline, which pollutes the air. Other vehicles are electric. But most of the electricity they use comes from burning coal, which pollutes the air, too.

Factory smoke

Spraying crops with chemicals

Roads produce air pollution and noise.

The world's biggest problem is overpopulation. There are over 5 billion people on Earth, and the number is growing fast.

Litter, oil spills, car exhaust fumes and factory waste are all types of pollution. Some pollution is just ugly. But it often contains dangerous chemicals, too. These can poison plants, animals, soil and even the atmosphere.

37

USEFUL WORDS

Avalanche Sudden slide of snow and ice down a mountainside.

Continent Large land mass.

Core Center of the Earth. There is an outer and an inner core.

Crust Outer surface of the Earth.

Desert Dry region with little rain.

Earthquake Sudden shaking of the Earth's surface.

Epicenter Point at which an earthquake starts.

Fault Large crack in the Earth's surface.

Focus Point on the surface closest to the epicenter of an earthquake.

Galaxy Group of stars and planets.

Glacier River of ice.

Jungle Thick forest in a warm part of the world.

Lightning Giant electric spark produced during thunderstorms.

Magma Liquid rock inside the Earth. It reaches the surface and becomes lava.

Mantle Inner layer of the Earth, between the crust and the core.

Milky Way The galaxy that includes the Earth and our solar system.

Richter scale Scale used to measure the size of earthquakes.

Solar system All the planets and other bodies that spin around the Sun.

Volcano Opening in the crust where liquid rock reaches the Earth's surface.

Wind Moving air.

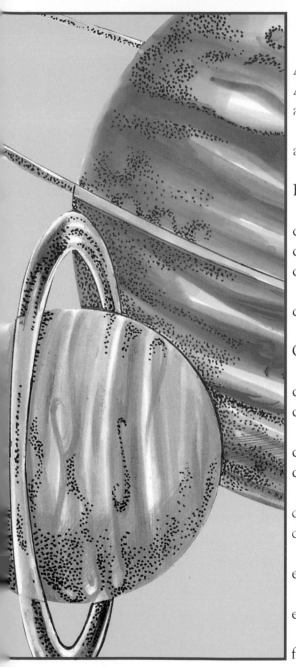

INDEX